HANDS AT THE NATIVITY

A Service for Advent or Christmas

by

Jean Froggett

British Library Cataloguing in Publication Data.
A catalogue record for this book is available from the British Library.

Royalties from this project are donated to The Leprosy Mission

ISBN 0 86071 591 4

Publisher
MOORLEY'S Print & Publishing
23 Park Rd., Ilkeston, Derbys DE7 5DA
Tel/Fax: (0115) 932 0643

HANDS AT THE NATIVITY

Taking part:

Leader
Bible Readers (or the Leader)
Characters:
A Shepherd
The Innkeeper's Wife
A Wise Man
King Herod
Mary, Mother of Jesus

Materials:

A large sheet of card on which a circle, bearing a coloured map of the world, or a copy of the world map provided later in this book (suitably enlarged and coloured), to be displayed on a board or wall before the Service begins.

Activity paper (different colours) for cut-outs of hands. A pair for each of the above characters, and if possible, a single hand each, for members of the congregation, to be placed on seats before the service begins, along with a supply of ballpoints or pencils.

Blu tack or similar adhesive.

HANDS AT THE NATIVITY
Part 1 – Script

Leader: Welcome to our Service of Carols and Readings, reminding us of the events of that first Christmas and their significance for us, and for the world today:

ALL: **Lord God, we come to you**
because in you we find our hope,
our joy, our peace.
We come to you
because in your beloved Son
you first came to us.
We come to give you thanks and praise
and to celebrate again, His birth.

Leader: Our first carol is "Hark the herald angels sing"

1st Bible Reading: Luke Ch 2 v. 8-13

Leader: A Shepherd speaks:

THE SHEPHERD
Mine are the hands of a working man;
A poor man - who spends his days and many a night
on the hills outside Bethlehem, in all kinds of weather.
My hands are big and the skin is leathery.
My fingers are gnarled and painful.
I use these hands to snatch the wet fleece
of sheep that have gone astray.
I lift heavy stones
that guard the entrance to the sheep fold.
But they are gentle hands too:
when ewes are giving birth
I gently ease the new born lamb
into this cold and hostile world
and place it close to the warmth of its mother.

That night when angels filled the heavens with their light,
I raised these strong, hardened hands to shield my eyes.
The sound of the angel voices echoed across the land,
bringing glad tidings of great joy
to us, poor shepherds, and to all mankind,
telling of the promised Saviour's birth.
Now I lift these hands in prayer,
and praise the God of our fathers,
for His wonderful gift,
the Lamb of God.

Leader: For those who, in this Present Age, hear and respond to the good news of the coming of our Saviour Jesus Christ:

ALL: **Thanks be to God.**

[The 'Shepherd' places the cut-outs of two hands on the rim of the globe]

Leader: The Innkeeper's wife speaks:

THE INNKEEPER'S WIFE
Many hands make light work - so they say.
I could have done with a dozen hands that night!
Our Inn was bursting at the seams;
the census in full swing,
every guest raising hands to demand this or that,
pointing and threatening
when their demands were not answered.
And then, *they* arrived.
The young couple, weary after their long journey,
wanting a room
and her big with child.
My husband wanted to turn them away,
but I couldn't find it in my heart to let them go.
Yes, I know it's not a suitable place to give birth,
but the stable was the best we could offer,
and they seemed glad to take it.

Then it all started.
'All hands to the pump', they say.
I had to run to the pump for water to boil.
It's a messy business
giving birth.
I know - I've done it four times
and it doesn't get any easier.
But this was her first - always the worst!
But she was brave, and so calm,
praying all the time.
My plump, warm hands helped
to rub her back and mop her brow.
And then - wonder of wonders,
among the water and the blood,
the child slipped into my hands.
At that moment . . .
I did not know I was holding
the Son of God.
Born like any other child,
but destined to be
the Saviour of the world.

[The 'Innkeeper's Wife' places the cut-outs of two hands on the rim of the globe]

Leader: For those who find in everyday tasks, opportunities for service in the name of Christ our Saviour:

ALL: **Thanks be to God.**

Leader: Let us now sing, "While shepherds watched their flocks"

Bible reading: Matthew Ch 2 verses 1, 2 and 9-11

Leader: A Wise Man speaks:

THE WISE MAN
My hands had fingered their way
through ancient books and charts.
They had held the glass to my eyes
to scan the heavens,
and there it was!
That special star - an omen
of a great and mighty wonder.
With my fellow astrologers,
I set out to find the Promised King.
The journey, over mountains and desert sands
took many hot and tiring days.
The meeting with Herod -
(we had to pay him the courtesy of a visit),
was a frightening affair.
But by the goodness and guidance of God
we escaped him,
and found the mother and child
in a stable.
In that unlikely place
we knew we were in the presence
of a new born King.
We knelt in homage.
My hands - hands that in my own country
held wisdom, might and power,
were now bearing a gift
to one, greater than I.
Gold was my gift,
a gift for a King, who would have
the wisdom and power of God
to work wonders
in the lives of all who came to Him.

[The 'Wise Man' places his cut-out hands on the rim of the globe]

Leader: For those whose learning and wisdom enriches our lives, in the arts, the sciences and in medicine:

ALL: **Thanks be to God.**

Leader: We'll now sing, "Once in Royal David's City"

Bible Reading: Matthew Ch 2 v. 16-18

Leader: King Herod speaks:

KING HEROD
My hands are the hands of a ruler,
a ruthless King.
They have dealt out injury and punishment.
One wave of MY hand, and orders are carried out.
I knew when those so-called Wise Men arrived
there was a problem looming.
A new King indeed! Huh!
I wasn't going to let a Jewish youngster take over my throne.
I have the Roman Emperor to answer to.
I have ruled this outpost
of the Roman Empire with an iron hand.
It was this hand that signed the decree -
"Kill every Hebrew child under the age of two."
The hand of evil that was copied
by every soldier brandishing his sword.
The swords that slaughtered innocent children
and broke the hearts of weeping mothers.
And those hands of evil
continue to work in the world.

['King Herod' places his cut-out hands round the globe.]

Leader: For those who plan and carry out evil; for those whose lives are wracked with guilt for past deeds, may the knowledge and love of Christ change their lives:

ALL: **Lord hear our prayer.**

Leader: Our next carol is "Silent Night"

Bible Reading: Luke Ch 2 v.30-33 and Luke Ch 2 v. 1-7

Leader: Mary speaks:

MARY
That particular day - the day that changed my life,
my hands were doing all the tasks
a young woman does -
the washing, baking, fetching water . . .
Yes, I was by the well
when he spoke to me.
I knew he was an angel,
I had never seen his like before.
"You have been chosen by God," he said.
I thought my mind was crazed by the heat.
My hands were wet with the cold, fresh water from the well,
I placed them over my forehead and eyes,
hoping to clear my head.
But the vision did not go away -
it was real.

And in that stable at Bethlehem,
my son was born.
No! Not just my son, but the Son of God.
As I held him in my arms
and caressed him gently with these hands,
I did not know what his future would be.
As I watched him, his tiny hands
reached out to me;
as they have done throughout his life
to the sick, the despised, the lonely.
And still he is reaching out
to bring the love of God
to all who need him
and will let him come into their hearts.
And at the end,

as he hung on the cross,
these hands, that had nurtured and cared for him,
they covered my eyes and face again,
this time - wet with tears.

['Mary' places her cut-out hands on the rim of the globe.]

Leader: For all who devote their lives to caring for others and remain faithful to the teaching and example of Christ our Lord:

ALL: **Thanks be to God.**

Leader: 'Hands' - all playing their part in the events of that first Christmas. But now we bring the theme to life in our own time.

[If desirable, the Leader, Minister or Preacher may add a few thoughts in a short address.

At this point in the service, the Leader may suggest that the organist plays 'Born in the Night' or other suitable music, whilst members of the congregation write on the coloured, cut-out hands, the names of persons or charities whose hands are caring or helpful, or the name of someone who needs caring hands, or someone to whom they wish to express thanks or a brief prayer. Depending on your situation these can be collected by stewards or held by the people to be added to the collage during the carol after the prayers.]

PRAYERS OF INTERCESSION

Loving Lord, you have called us to be your witnesses and your hands in the world.

We pray for:
those overwhelmed by worry and grief;
those for whom this Christmas season will be a time of loneliness;
those who are weary because of the needs and demands of others;

Grant us Lord, the strength and understanding to meet the needs of those around us.
Lord of the loving hands:

All: **Hear our prayer.**

Leader: We pray for the hungry, the displaced and homeless in African countries and areas around the world that have suffered natural disasters;
for men and women worldwide, striving to maintain their Christian witness in the face of intimidation and persecution;
for families bereaved and children orphaned by Aids, and for those who struggle to care for them;
for those who, as a result of war or violence have lost limbs and are unable to work to support their family;
Lord of the loving heart:

ALL: **Hear our prayer.**

Leader: At this busy time of year, we pray for those who will have to work over Christmas to keep us safe, warm and well:
for those on duty in hospitals, the fire service and the police;
for carers of individuals in their own homes, and in residential homes;
for those who transport and ensure our supply of food;
for those serving in the Forces to maintain peace, and restore communities;
Lord, whose hands showed justice and mercy:

ALL: **Hear our prayer.**

ALL: **Loving God, we praise you**
for the events of that first Christmas:
for Mary, who accepted the responsibility
of giving birth and caring for
the Saviour of the World;

for the message of the angels,
bringing good news to all people;
for the shepherds, who came to welcome
the Shepherd of the humble and poor;
for the Wise Men, who sought the Child,
bringing gifts, to show the meaning
of His birth, His life, His death and resurrection.
Grant that having heard the story again,
we may respond with gratitude,
with love and willing hands
to meet the needs of those around us,
and those across the world whose lives are
blighted by sickness, violence and poverty.
Merciful Lord, hear our prayer. Amen.

Leader: The paper hands that we have personalised will be added to our collage as we sing, "O come all ye faithful".

(Offertory may be taken during the singing of this hymn, and two volunteers, using blu tack or similar, arrange the collected 'hands' or assist the congregation to fill the remaining space round the globe.)

Leader: Let us dedicate the thoughts and prayers shown on the display of 'Hands':

ALL: **Lord Jesus Christ**
let the love you brought into the world
be born anew in our hearts,
and may the peace you promised
come to those
whose lives are broken
by uncertainty, fear, injustice and war. Amen.

ALL: **We go in the power of the Spirit, to bring glory to God,**
to take the Love of Christ into every part of our life,
and the lives of all we meet.

Part 2 – Photocopiable Material

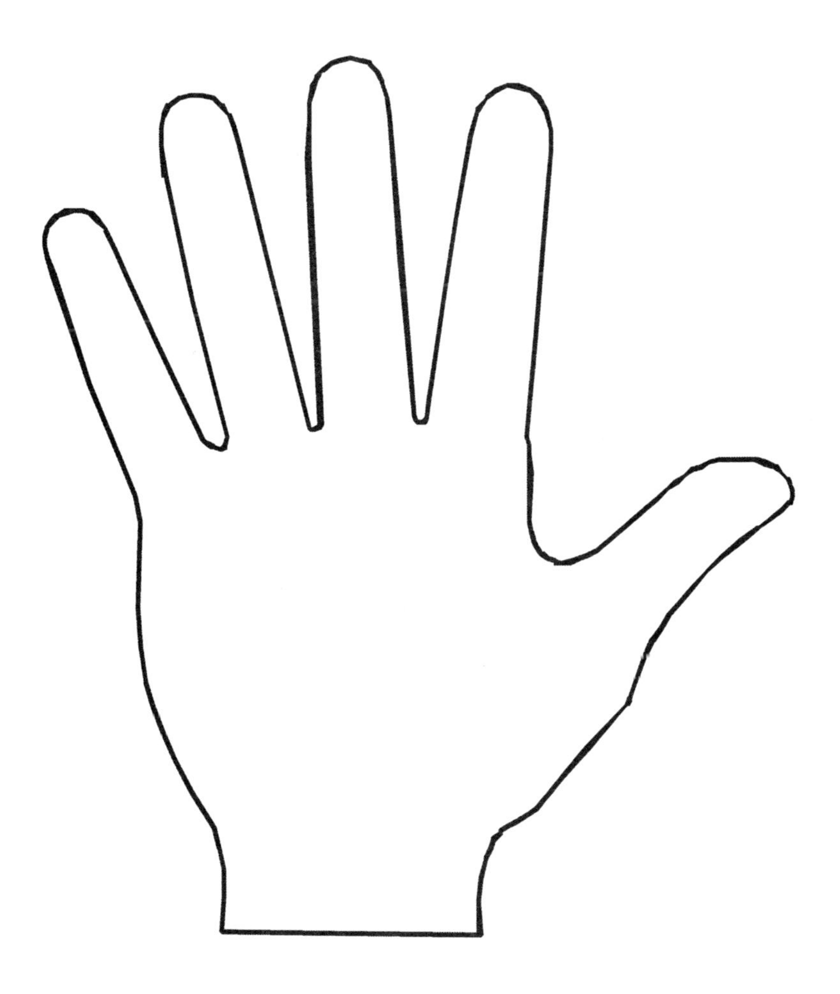

Either cut out this hand to use as a template or use as a copying master

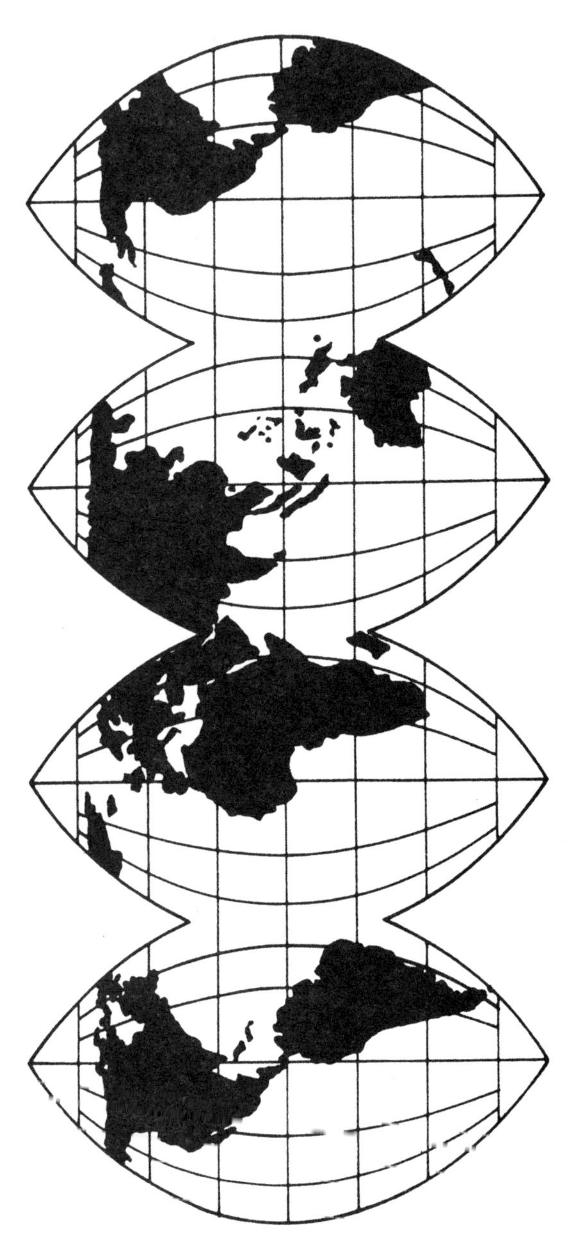

We suggest that you enlarge this map on a photocopier (A5 > A3 i.e. 200% will reproduce this on A3 paper). Add colour for better effect.

HANDS AT THE NATIVITY
Order of Service

Leader: Welcome to our Service of Carols and readings, reminding us of the events of that first Christmas and their significance for us, and for the world today:

ALL: **Lord God, we come to you**
because in you we find our hope,
our joy, our peace.
We come to you
because in your beloved Son
you first came to us.
We come to give you thanks and praise
and to celebrate again, His birth.

Hark the herald angels sing

Hark! The herald-angels sing
Glory to the new-born King,
Peace on earth, and mercy mild,
God and sinners reconciled.
Joyful, all ye nations, rise
Join the triumph of the skies;
With the angelic host proclaim:
'Christ is born in Bethlehem'.

Hark! The herald-angels sing
Glory to the new-born King.

Christ, by highest heaven adored,
Christ, the everlasting Lord,
Late in time behold him come,
Offspring of a virgin's womb.
Veiled in flesh the Godhead see!
Hail, the incarnate Deity!
Pleased as man with men to dwell,
Jesus, our Immanuel:

Hail, the heaven-born Prince of Peace!
Hail, the Sun of Righteousness!
Light and life to all he brings,
Risen with healing in his wings.
Mild he lays his glory by,
Born that man no more may die,
Born to raise the sons of earth,
Born to give them second birth:

Bible Reading:

THE SHEPHERD

Leader: For those who, in this present Age, hear and respond to the good news of the coming of our Saviour Jesus Christ:

ALL: **Thanks be to God.**

THE INNKEEPER'S WIFE

Leader: For those who find in everyday tasks, opportunities for service in the name of Christ our Saviour:

ALL: **Thanks be to God.**

While shepherds watched their flocks

While shepherds watched their flocks by night,
All seated on the ground,
The angel of the Lord came down,
And glory shone around.

'Fear not,' said he (for mighty dread
Had seized their troubled mind)
'Glad tidings of great joy I bring
To you and all mankind.

'To you in David's town this day
Is born of David's line
A Saviour, who is Christ the Lord;
And this shall be the sign.

'The heavenly Babe you there shall find
To human view displayed,
All meanly wrapped in swaddling bands,
And in a manger laid.'

Thus spake the seraph; and forthwith
Appeared a shining throng
Of angels praising God, and thus
Addressed their joyful song:

'All glory be to God on high,
And to the earth be peace;
Goodwill henceforth from heaven to men
Begin and never cease.'

Bible Reading:

THE WISE MAN

Leader: For those whose learning and wisdom enriches our lives, in the arts, the sciences and in medicine:

ALL: **Thanks be to God.**

Once in Royal David's City

Once in royal David's city
Stood a lowly cattle-shed,
Where a mother laid her baby
In a manger for his bed:
Mary was that mother mild,
Jesus Christ her little child.

He came down to earth from heaven
Who is God and Lord of all,
And his shelter was a stable,
And his cradle was a stall;
With the poor and mean and lowly
Lived on earth our Saviour holy.

And through all his wondrous childhood
He would honour and obey,
Love, and watch the lowly maiden
In whose gentle arms he lay.
Christian children all must be
Mild, obedient, good as he.

For he is our childhood's pattern,
Day by day like us he grew,
He was little, weak, and helpless,
Tears and smiles like us he knew;
And he feeleth for our sadness,
And he shareth in our gladness.

And our eyes at last shall see him,
Through his own redeeming love,
For that child so dear and gentle
Is our Lord in heaven above;
And he leads his children on
To the place where he is gone.

Not in that poor lowly stable,
With the oxen standing by,
We shall see him; but in heaven,
Set at God's right hand on high;
When like stars his children crowned
All in white shall wait around.

Bible Reading:

KING HEROD

Leader: For those who plan and carry out evil; for those whose lives are wracked with guilt for past deeds, may the knowledge and love of Christ change their lives:

ALL: **Lord hear our prayer.**

Silent Night

Silent night, holy night:
Sleeps the world; hid from sight,
Mary and Joseph in stable bare
Watch o'er the child belovéd and fair
Sleeping in heavenly rest.

Silent night, holy night:
Shepherds first saw the light,
Heard resounding clear and long,
Far and near, the angel-song:
'Christ the Redeemer is here!'

Silent night, holy night:
Son of God, O how bright
Love is smiling from thy face!
Strikes for us now the hour of grace,
Saviour, since thou art born.

Bible Reading:

MARY

Leader: For all who devote their lives to caring for others and remain faithful to the teaching and example of Christ our Lord:

ALL: **Thanks be to God.**

Leader: 'Hands' - all playing their part in the events of that first Christmas. But now we bring the theme to life in our own time.

As music plays members of the congregation are asked to write on the coloured, cut-out hands, the names of persons or charities whose hands are caring or helpful, or the name of someone who needs caring hands, or someone to whom they wish to express thanks or a brief prayer.

PRAYERS OF INTERCESSION

Leader: . . . .Lord of the loving hands:

All: **Hear our prayer.**

Leader: . . . Lord of the loving heart:

ALL: **Hear our prayer.**

Leader: . . . Lord, whose hands showed justice and mercy:

ALL: **Hear our prayer.**

ALL: **Loving God, we praise you**
for the events of that first Christmas:
for Mary, who accepted the responsibility
of giving birth and caring for
the Saviour of the World;
for the message of the angels,
bringing good news to all people;
for the shepherds, who came to welcome
the Shepherd of the humble and poor;
for the Wise Men, who sought the Child
bringing gifts, to show the meaning
of His birth, His life, His death and resurrection.
Grant that having heard the story again,
we may respond with gratitude,
with love and willing hands
to meet the needs of those around us,
and those across the world whose lives are
blighted by sickness, violence and poverty.
Merciful Lord, hear our prayer. Amen.

O come all ye faithful

O come, all ye faithful,
Joyful and triumphant,
O come ye, O come ye to Bethlehem;
Come and behold him,
Born the King of angels:

O come, let us adore him,(x3) Christ the Lord.

True God of true God,
Light of Light eternal,
Lo, he abhors not the virgin's womb;
Son of the Father,
Begotten, not created:

See how the shepherds,
Summoned to his cradle,
Leaving their flocks, draw night to gaze;
We too will thither
Bend our joyful footsteps:

Lo, star-led chieftains,
Magi, Christ adoring,
Offer him incense, gold, and myrrh;
We to the Christ-child
Bring our hearts' oblations:

Sing, choirs of angels,
Sing in exultation,
Sing, all ye citizens of heaven above:
'Glory to God
In the highest':

(Christmas Day)

Yea, Lord, we greet thee,
Born this happy morning,
Jesus, to thee be glory given:
Word of the Father,
Now in flesh appearing:

Offertory

Leader: Let us dedicate the thoughts and prayers shown on the display of 'Hands' :

ALL: **Lord Jesus Christ**
let the love you brought into the world
be born anew in our hearts,
and may the peace you promised
come to those
whose lives are broken
by uncertainty, fear, injustice and war. Amen.

ALL: **We go in the power of the Spirit, to bring glory to God,**
to take the Love of Christ into every part of our life,
and the lives of all we meet.

HINTS FOR COPYING YOUR ORDER OF SERVICE

1. Carefully cut out pages 15 – 29 maintaining margins as in the book.
2. White out the page numbers (15 – 29) leaving the numbers 1 – 8 for your Order of Service.
3. Fold four pieces of thin A4 exactly in half (A5) then open out to A4 again.
4. Take the first sheet and with a little Pritt (or similar glue) on each corner of the back of page 1 position it on the right side of your sheet. Now take page 8, glue and affix to the left half of your sheet.
5. Take second sheet, follow same procedure but with page 2 on left and 7 on right.
6. Take third sheet for page 3 on right and page 6 on left.
7. Take fourth sheet for page 4 on left and page 5 on right.
8. Using the "Copy on both sides" function of the Copier print the first sheet backed by the second
9. Repeat no 8 backing the third sheet with the fourth sheet.
10. Collate and fold in half to give you an eight page A5 Order of Service.